Date: 2/29/16

J BIO BRADY
Gordon, Nick,
Tom Brady/

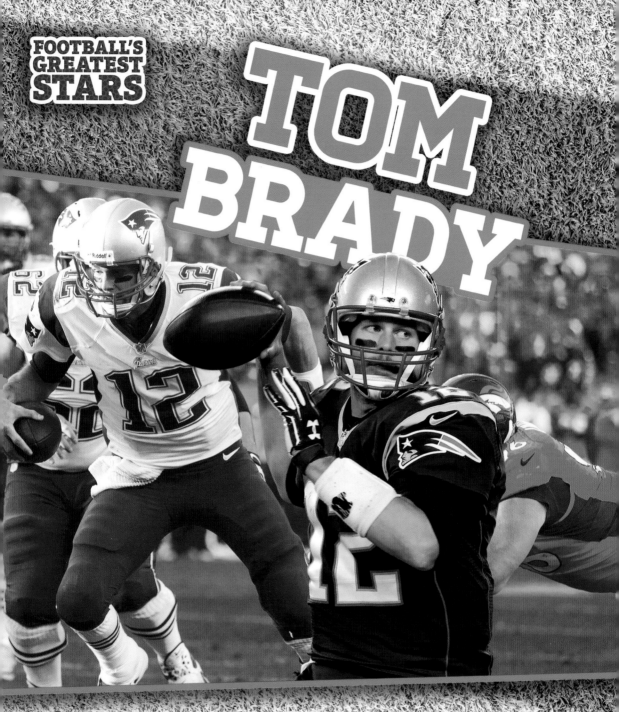

FOOTBALL'S GREATEST STARS

TOM BRADY

by Nick Gordon

SportsZone
An Imprint of Abdo Publishing
abdopublishing.com

abdopublishing.com

Published by Abdo Publishing, a division of ABDO, PO Box 398166, Minneapolis, Minnesota 55439. Copyright © 2016 by Abdo Consulting Group, Inc. International copyrights reserved in all countries. No part of this book may be reproduced in any form without written permission from the publisher. SportsZone™ is a trademark and logo of Abdo Publishing.

Printed in the United States of America, North Mankato, Minnesota
042015
092015

Cover Photos: Aaron M. Sprecher/AP Images (foreground); Damian Strohmeyer/AP Images (background)
Interior Photos: Aaron M. Sprecher/AP Images 1 (foreground); Damian Strohmeyer/AP Images 1 (background); Tom DiPace/AP Images, 4-5, 6; James D. Smith/Icon Sportswire, 7; Scott Boehm/AP Images, 8-9; Scott Audette/AP Images, 10; Duane Burleson/AP Images, 11; Daniel Mears/The Detroit News/AP Images, 12; Paul Warner/AP Images, 13; Bob Falcetti/Icon Sportswire, 14-15; Doug Mills/AP Images, 16-17; G. Newman Lowrance/AP Images, 18-19; David Duprey/AP Images, 20-21; Charles Krupa/AP Images, 22-23; Aaron M. Sprecher/AP Images, 24-25; Ben Liebenberg/AP Images, 26-27; Gene Lower/AP Images, 28-29

Editor: Nick Rebman
Series Designer: Jake Nordby

Library of Congress Control Number: 2015932398

Cataloging-in-Publication Data
Gordon, Nick.
 Tom Brady / Nick Gordon.
   p. cm. -- (Football's greatest stars)
Includes index.
ISBN 978-1-62403-824-2
1. Brady, Tom, 1977- --Juvenile literature. 2. Football players--United States--Biography--Juvenile literature. 3. Quarterbacks (Football)--United States--Biography--Juvenile literature.   I. Title.
796.332092--dc23
[B]   2015932398

CONTENTS

SUPER BOWL STUNNER

Few people gave the New England Patriots a chance to win the 2002 Super Bowl. They were facing the powerful St. Louis Rams. The Patriots were led by young quarterback Tom Brady. Before the season, most fans had not known who Brady was. Now he was playing in the biggest game of the year.

The Rams tied the game with 1:30 to go in the fourth quarter. Brady led his offense onto the field.

FAST FACT
The Patriots were the first Super Bowl team to choose to be introduced as a group. Before that, players were introduced individually.

4

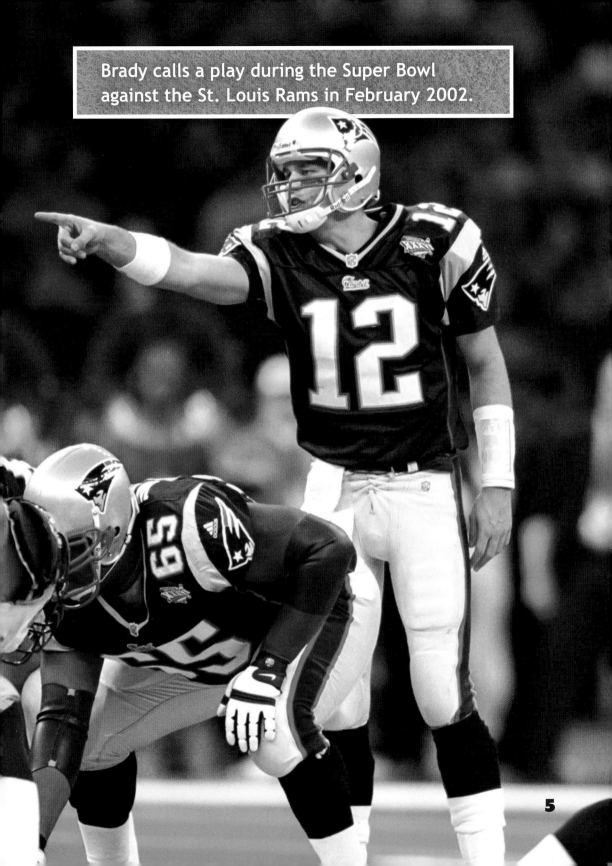

Brady calls a play during the Super Bowl against the St. Louis Rams in February 2002.

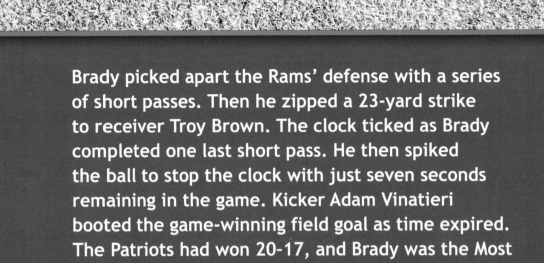

Brady picked apart the Rams' defense with a series of short passes. Then he zipped a 23-yard strike to receiver Troy Brown. The clock ticked as Brady completed one last short pass. He then spiked the ball to stop the clock with just seven seconds remaining in the game. Kicker Adam Vinatieri booted the game-winning field goal as time expired. The Patriots had won 20-17, and Brady was the Most Valuable Player (MVP)!

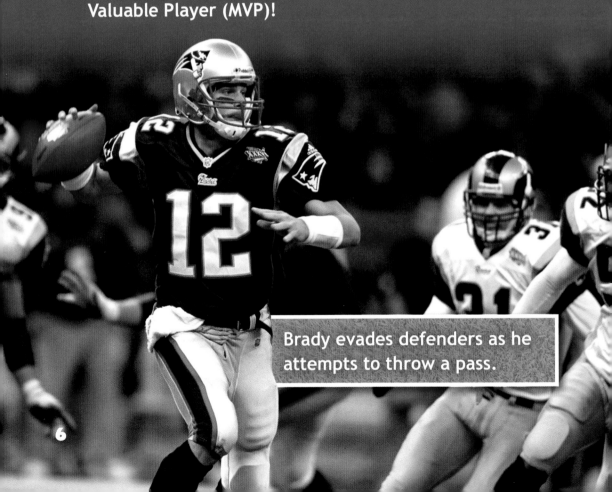

Brady evades defenders as he attempts to throw a pass.

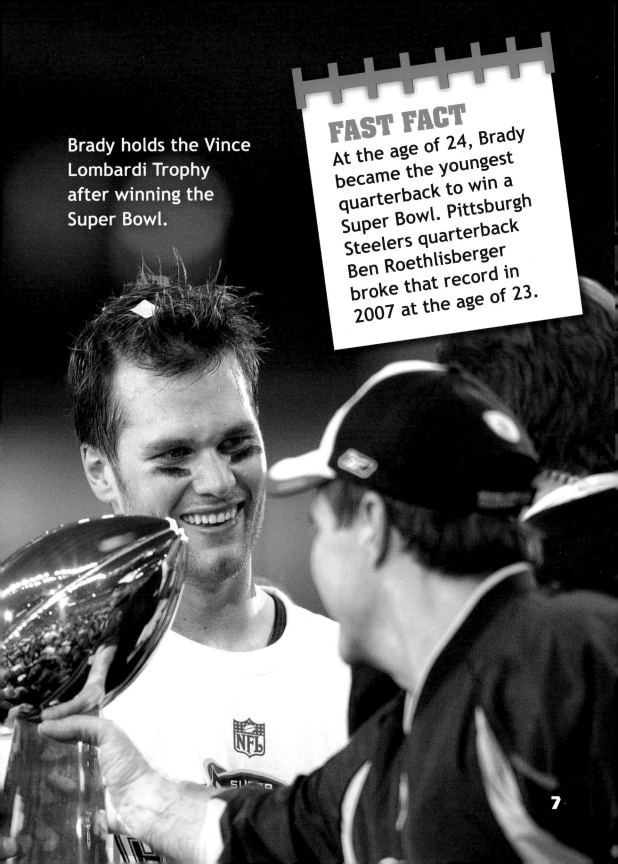

Brady holds the Vince Lombardi Trophy after winning the Super Bowl.

At the age of 24, Brady became the youngest quarterback to win a Super Bowl. Pittsburgh Steelers quarterback Ben Roethlisberger broke that record in 2007 at the age of 23.

YOUNG TOM BRADY

Tom Brady was born on August 3, 1977, in San Mateo, California. He loved football. He cheered for Joe Montana and the San Francisco 49ers as a child.

In high school, Tom was the star of both the baseball and football teams. He graduated in 1995. The Montreal Expos drafted him in baseball's amateur draft that year. But Tom turned down the contract offer. He wanted to play football.

FAST FACT

Brady played catcher on his high school's baseball team.

Brady prepares to take a snap in a 1999 game against the Indiana Hoosiers.

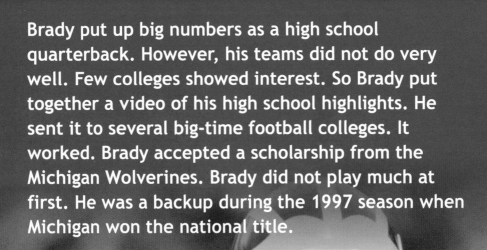

Brady put up big numbers as a high school quarterback. However, his teams did not do very well. Few colleges showed interest. So Brady put together a video of his high school highlights. He sent it to several big-time football colleges. It worked. Brady accepted a scholarship from the Michigan Wolverines. Brady did not play much at first. He was a backup during the 1997 season when Michigan won the national title.

Brady warms up in a practice before the Citrus Bowl.

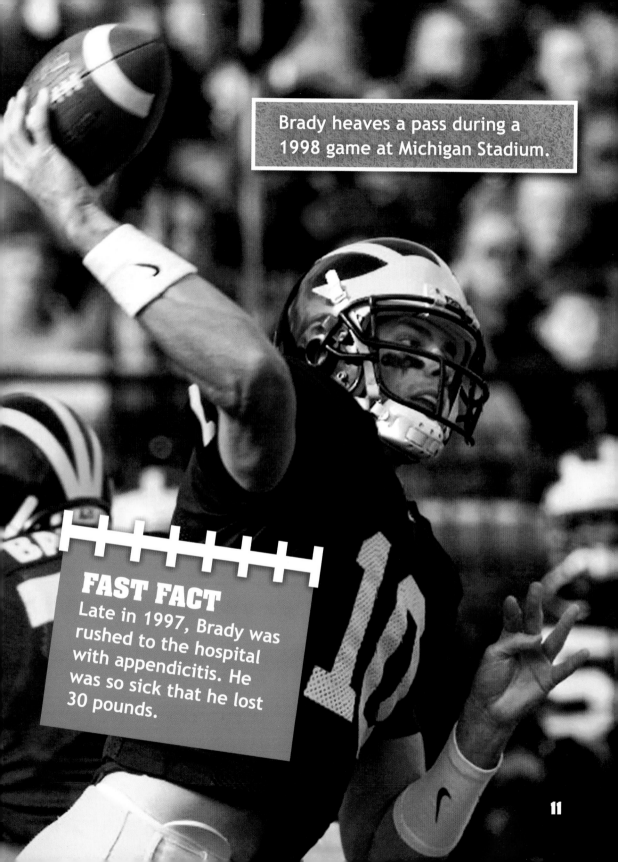

Brady heaves a pass during a 1998 game at Michigan Stadium.

FAST FACT

Late in 1997, Brady was rushed to the hospital with appendicitis. He was so sick that he lost 30 pounds.

Brady started to get playing time in 1998. At first he split time with fellow quarterback Drew Henson. But by the end of the season, Brady had taken over as the main passer. He led the Wolverines to a 45-31 victory over Arkansas in the Citrus Bowl.

Brady and the Wolverines finished the 1999 regular season ranked eighth in the nation. Brady then led his team to a thrilling comeback victory over Alabama in the Orange Bowl.

Brady passes the ball during the Wolverines' victory in the Orange Bowl.

Brady in action against
Michigan State in 1999

FAST FACT
Brady set Orange Bowl
records with 369
passing yards and four
touchdowns.

FROM BACKUP TO STAR

Many National Football League (NFL) scouts were not impressed with Brady. They liked his arm strength, but they thought he was too slow-footed. One draft expert said Brady "didn't have the total package of skills."

Brady watched the 2000 NFL Draft, waiting for his phone to ring. Finally, the Patriots called. They selected him in the sixth round. Brady was the 199th player chosen.

FAST FACT
Brady was the seventh quarterback chosen in the 2000 NFL Draft.

Brady plays in a game against the New York Jets during the 2001 season.

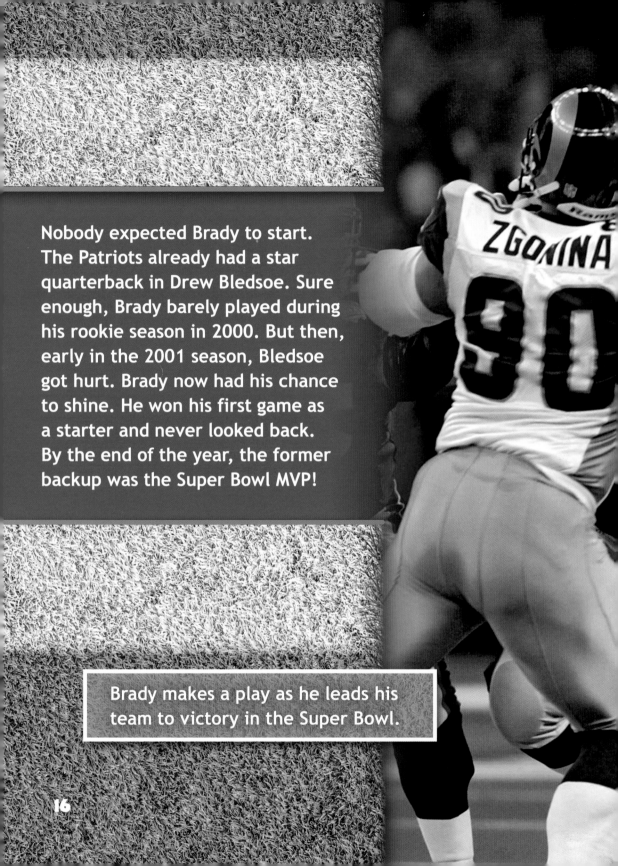

Nobody expected Brady to start. The Patriots already had a star quarterback in Drew Bledsoe. Sure enough, Brady barely played during his rookie season in 2000. But then, early in the 2001 season, Bledsoe got hurt. Brady now had his chance to shine. He won his first game as a starter and never looked back. By the end of the year, the former backup was the Super Bowl MVP!

Brady makes a play as he leads his team to victory in the Super Bowl.

FAST FACT

Brady's first career start came against quarterback Peyton Manning and the Indianapolis Colts. Manning and Brady went on to become two of the greatest quarterbacks in NFL history.

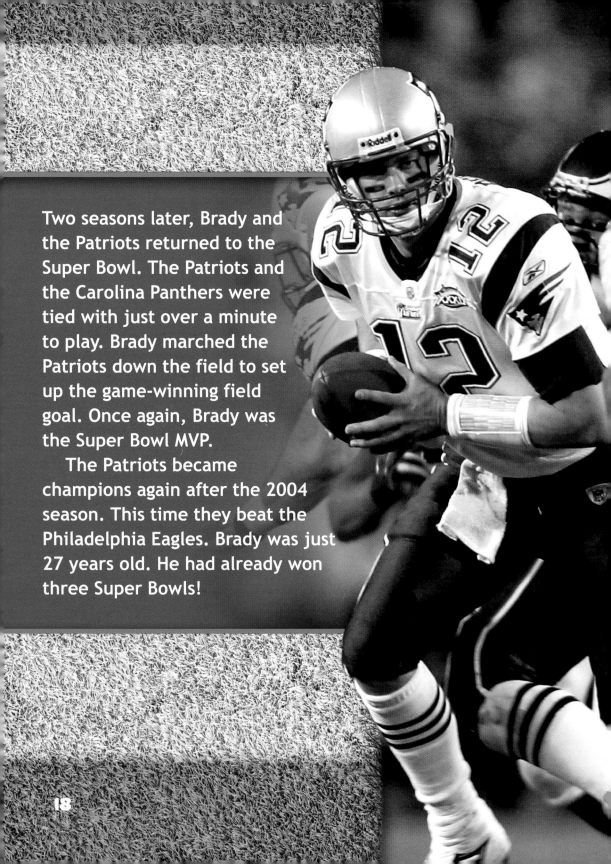

Two seasons later, Brady and the Patriots returned to the Super Bowl. The Patriots and the Carolina Panthers were tied with just over a minute to play. Brady marched the Patriots down the field to set up the game-winning field goal. Once again, Brady was the Super Bowl MVP.

The Patriots became champions again after the 2004 season. This time they beat the Philadelphia Eagles. Brady was just 27 years old. He had already won three Super Bowls!

Brady hands off the ball during the Super Bowl in February 2005.

RECORDS AND LETDOWNS

Brady and the Patriots remained one of the NFL's top teams. But they could not recapture their playoff magic. The Patriots blew a big lead over the Indianapolis Colts in the AFC Championship Game in January 2007.

The 2007 regular season was magical. Brady was named the NFL's MVP. He set an NFL record by throwing 50 touchdown passes. The Patriots finished the regular season with a perfect 16-0 record. However, the New York Giants stunned them with a late touchdown to win the Super Bowl.

FAST FACT

The Miami Dolphins achieved a perfect season, including a Super Bowl win, in 1972.

New York Giants defenders take down Brady during the Super Bowl in February 2008.

Brady suffered a season-ending knee injury in the first game of the 2008 season. But he came back strong in 2009. He was named the NFL Comeback Player of the Year. Then in 2010, he won his second league MVP award.

Brady and the Patriots were hot in the 2011 playoffs. Brady threw a playoff-record six touchdown passes against the Denver Broncos. The Patriots advanced to the Super Bowl. But again, the Giants beat them with a late touchdown.

FAST FACT
Brady married supermodel Gisele Bündchen in 2009.

Brady runs the ball against the New York Jets in 2009.

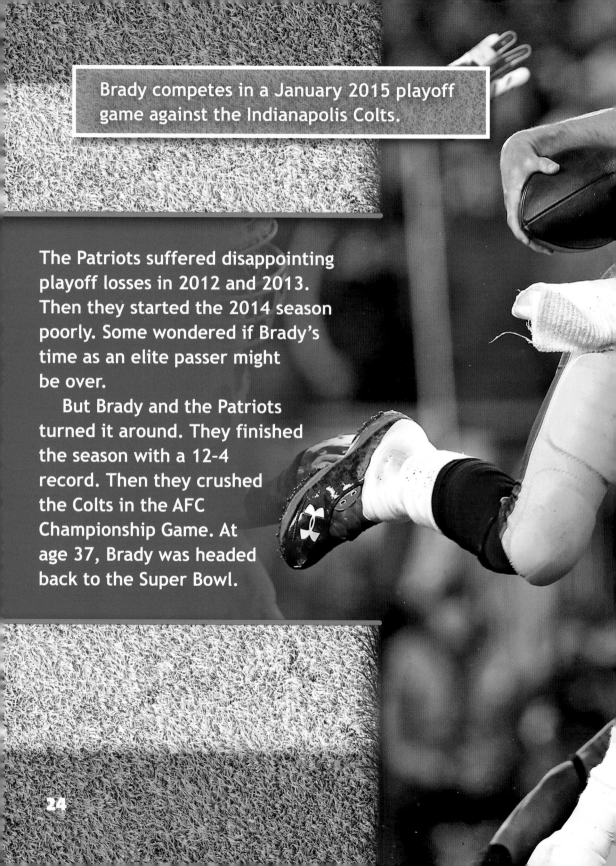

Brady competes in a January 2015 playoff game against the Indianapolis Colts.

The Patriots suffered disappointing playoff losses in 2012 and 2013. Then they started the 2014 season poorly. Some wondered if Brady's time as an elite passer might be over.

But Brady and the Patriots turned it around. They finished the season with a 12-4 record. Then they crushed the Colts in the AFC Championship Game. At age 37, Brady was headed back to the Super Bowl.

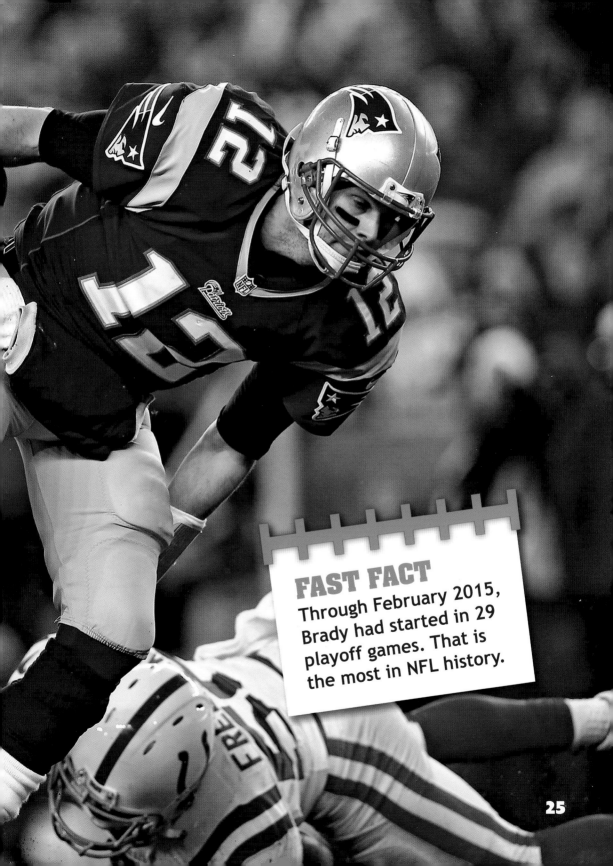

FAST FACT
Through February 2015, Brady had started in 29 playoff games. That is the most in NFL history.

CHAMPION AGAIN

The 2015 Super Bowl was a classic. The Patriots faced the defending champion Seattle Seahawks. Seattle built a 24-14 lead. Then Brady took over. He hit Danny Amendola with a short touchdown pass. With two minutes to play, Brady connected with Julian Edelman for another score. The Patriots led 28-24.

Seattle drove the ball down to New England's 1-yard line. But then Seattle quarterback Russell Wilson threw an interception. The game was over, and Brady was once again a champion!

FAST FACT
With the win in 2015, Brady joined Joe Montana and Terry Bradshaw as the only quarterbacks to win four Super Bowls.

Brady scans the field during the Super Bowl in February 2015.

Who is the greatest quarterback of all time? It is a question fans love to debate. However, many feel that Brady's 2015 Super Bowl victory put an end to the debate. Throughout his career, he has guided his teams to six Super Bowls and won four. Both are records.

Brady was all but overlooked when he entered the NFL in 2000. When he leaves the game, he will exit as a legend.

FAST FACT
In 2015, Brady set the all-time record for most career postseason touchdown passes.

Brady celebrates his fourth Super Bowl victory after defeating the Seattle Seahawks.

TIMELINE

1977

Tom Brady is born on August 3 in San Mateo, California.

1995

Brady turns down a contract with the Montreal Expos and accepts a football scholarship from Michigan.

2000

After the 1999 season, Brady leads Michigan to an Orange Bowl victory. The New England Patriots select him in the sixth round of the NFL draft.

2001

Brady takes over for injured quarterback Drew Bledsoe and goes on to lead the Patriots to a Super Bowl victory.

2005

After the 2004 season, Brady and the Patriots win their third Super Bowl in four years.

2007

Brady and the Patriots post a perfect 16-0 regular season but go on to lose the Super Bowl to the New York Giants.

2012

After the 2011 season, the Patriots again lose the Super Bowl to the Giants.

2015

After the 2014 season, the Patriots defeat the Seattle Seahawks to win the Super Bowl. Brady is named Super Bowl MVP.

GLOSSARY

AMATEUR
Someone who is not paid to perform an activity.

APPENDICITIS
A condition in which the appendix becomes inflamed and painful.

CONTRACT
An agreement to play for a certain team.

ELITE
One of the very best.

SCHOLARSHIP
Money given to a student to pay for education expenses.

SCOUT
A person whose job is to look for talented young players.

INDEX

ABOUT THE AUTHOR

Nick Gordon is a lifelong football fan who lives in Maui, where he enjoys surfing, hiking, and writing on a sunny beach.